My first...

Visit to the Doctor

First published in the UK in 2009 by
QED Publishing
A Quarto Group Company
226 City Road
London EC1V 2TT
www.qed-publishing.co.uk

A catalogue record for this book is available
from the British Library.

ISBN 978 1 84835 257 5

Author Eve Marleau
Illustrator Michael Garton
Consultants Shirley Bickler and Tracey Dils
Designer Elaine Wilkinson

Publisher Steve Evans
Creative Director Zeta Davies
Managing Editor Amanda Askew

Printed and bound in China

The words in **bold** are
explained in the glossary
on page 24.

My First...
Visit to the Doctor

Eve Marleau and Michael Garton

QED Publishing

Jamie wakes up for school.
He doesn't feel very well.

"Mum, my throat hurts."

"Let me have a look at you." Mum touches Jamie's head with her hand. "You do feel hot. I'll call the doctor's **surgery**."

"We're seeing Dr Douglas at 11 o'clock."

Mum gives Jamie a big, warm jumper to wear.

Jamie gets into the car with Scruffy Ted.

Mum and Jamie sit down in the waiting room with the other patients.

Mr Roberts has a sore leg.

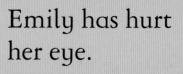

Emily has hurt her eye.

And Mrs Bengani has
a very sore neck!

"How did you hurt your
neck, Mrs Bengani?"

"I was driving in my car when
someone bumped into me," she says.

"Hello Jamie. I'm ready to see you now," says Dr Douglas.

Jamie looks around
Dr Douglas's room.

AS
XOE
TVHBC
AHMGBT
HRBKEANW

There is an eye chart on the
wall, a bed behind a blue
curtain and a desk.

11

"What's wrong, Jamie?"
"I have a sore throat."

"First, I'll take your **temperature** with a **thermometer**.

Next, I'll look in your ears with a tiny torch called an **otoscope**."

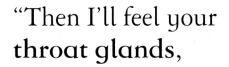

"Then I'll feel your **throat glands,**

and put a wooden stick on your tongue so I can check your throat."

"Say AhhhH!"

13

"Jamie, you have a throat **infection**.
You'll have to take some **medicine**."

14

Dr Douglas prints out the **prescription** from the computer.

"Please get this medicine from the chemist," he tells Mum.

Mum and Jamie go to the chemist to get the medicine.

Miss Granger gives Mum a small bottle of liquid. "This will make you feel better."

When they get home, Mum reads
the instructions on the bottle.

"You need to take two spoonfuls three times a day."

"Open wide!" she says.

Jamie and Scruffy Ted
spend the day resting.

He goes to sleep on the sofa.

Then Mum
brings Jamie
some soup.

When Dad gets home, Jamie
wriggles out from under his blanket.

"How are you feeling? Are you well enough
to eat some ice cream?" Dad asks.

"Dr Douglas said I had a throat infection. I think the ice cream will make me feel much better, thanks!"

Glossary

Infection A disease that affects a certain part of your body.

Medicine A liquid or pill that makes you feel better.

Otoscope A piece of equipment used to look inside the ears.

Prescription A piece of paper from the doctor that says what medicine you need.

Surgery A place where a doctor gives treatment to patients.

Temperature How hot or cold something is.

Thermometer Equipment that measures your temperature.

Throat gland An organ in the throat that produces spit.